Tales Near and Far

Ron Benson
Lynn Bryan
Kim Newlove
Liz Stenson
Iris Zammit

CONSULTANTS
Lillian Blakey
Florence Brown
Estella Clayton
Kathyrn D'Angelo
Susan Elliott-Johns
Charolette Player
Shari Schwartz
Lynn Swanson
Helen Tomassini
Debbie Toope

Prentice Hall Ginn

Contents

Rhyming Tales — 3
Hugh, Hugh by Dennis Lee
Susie and the Crocodile
by Sharon Stewart

Too Much Talk — 5
African folk tale
by Angela Shelf Medearis

The Legend of Hua Mu-lan — 12
Chinese legend retold by
Lucille Lui-Wong

A Fairy Tale Comes True — 20
newspaper article
by Lynn Blanche

Rumpelstiltskin — 23
play adapted from the
fairy tale by Shauna McLeod

Nadine's Writing
recount

Rhyming Tales

Illustrated by Mireille Levert

Hugh, Hugh

by Dennis Lee

Hugh, Hugh,
  At the age of two,
Built his house in a big brown shoe.
  Hugh, Hugh,
    What'll you do?
There's holes in the soles
And the rain comes through!

Susie and the Crocodile

by Sharon Stewart

Down beside the River Nile
Susie met a crocodile.

It wanted lunch, and wasn't choosy.
It thought it just might eat up Susie!

Its teeth were sharp, its jaws were wide.
She didn't wait to see inside.

She took off faster than a jet.
For all I know, she's running yet!

Too Much Talk

by Angela Shelf Medearis
Illustrated by Stefano Vitale

One day a farmer in West Africa went out to gather some yams. While he was digging, a yam said to him, "You did not water me. You did not weed me. And here you come to dig me up!"
"Well!" said the farmer. First he looked around. Then he looked at his dog and said, "Were you talking to me?"
"No," barked the dog. "It was the yam."

"**Aiyeee!**" screamed the farmer. He ran and he ran, uphill and downhill. And he ran and he ran, downhill and uphill. He ran until he met a man who was carrying some fish.

"Why are you running in the heat of the day?" said the fisher.

"Well," said the farmer, "first my yam talked and then my dog talked!"

"Oh," said the fisher, "that can't happen."

"Oh, yes it can," the fish said to them.

"**Aiyeee!**" screamed the farmer and the fisher. They ran and they ran, uphill and downhill. And they ran and they ran, downhill and uphill. They ran until they met a man who was weaving some cloth.

"Why are you running in the heat of the day?" the weaver said.

"Well," said the farmer, "first my yam talked, then my dog talked, and then the fish talked."

"Oh," said the weaver, "that can't happen."

"Oh, yes it can," the cloth said to them.

"**Aiyeee!**" screamed the farmer and the fisher and the weaver. They ran and they ran, uphill and downhill. And they ran and they ran, downhill and uphill. They ran until they came to a woman who was swimming.

"Ahhh," said the swimmer as she glided through the water. "Why are you running in the heat of the day?"

"Well," said the farmer, "first my yam talked, then my dog talked, then the fish talked, and then the cloth talked."

"Oh," said the swimmer as she did the backstroke, "that can't happen."

"Oh, yes it can," the water said to her.

"**Aiyeee!**" screamed the farmer and the fisher, the weaver and the swimmer. They ran and they ran, uphill and downhill. And they ran and they ran, downhill and uphill. They ran until they came to the house of the chief.

The chief came out and sat on his royal chair. He said to them, "Why are you running in the heat of the day?"

"Well," said the farmer, "first my yam talked, then my dog talked, then the fish talked, then the cloth talked, and then the water talked."

"Talk, talk, talk!" said the chief. "Too much talk! Yams don't talk! Fish don't talk! Cloth doesn't talk! And water doesn't talk! All this foolish talk will disturb the village! Go away, before I throw you in jail!"
So they all ran away.
"Imagine," said the chief, "a talking yam! How can that be?"
"So true," said the chair. "Whoever heard of a talking yam?"

"**Aiyeee!**" screamed the chief. And he ran uphill and downhill and was never seen again.

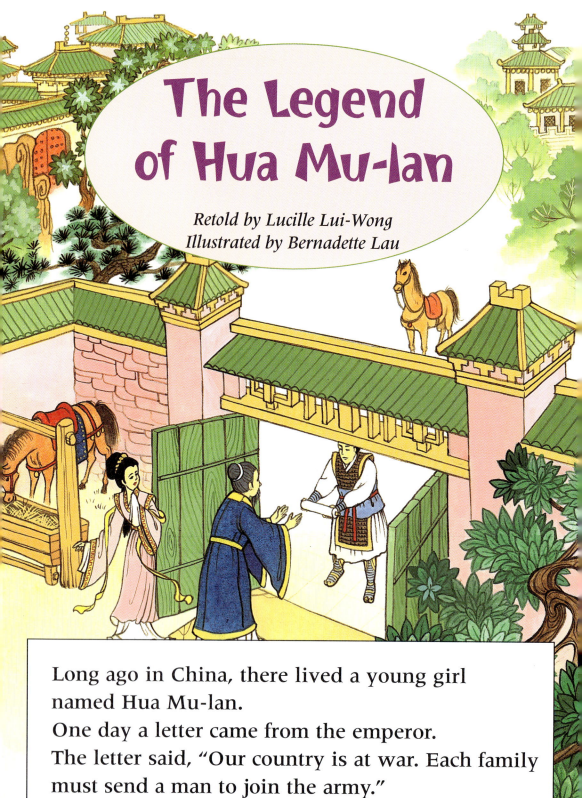

The Legend of Hua Mu-lan

Retold by Lucille Lui-Wong
Illustrated by Bernadette Lau

Long ago in China, there lived a young girl named Hua Mu-lan.
One day a letter came from the emperor.
The letter said, "Our country is at war. Each family must send a man to join the army."

Mu-lan was worried. Her father was
the only man in the house and he was
too old and weak to go to war. Then she had an idea.
"I will take your place and join the army," she told
her father. He sadly agreed.

Mu-lan bought a horse and saddle and a whip.
She dressed in heavy armour and carried
a sword and spear at her side.
She said goodbye to her family and left her home
to be a soldier in the emperor's army.

Some months later, Mu-lan and ten thousand soldiers rode along the banks of the Yellow River.
They camped in the snow under the moon.

Early one morning, Mu-lan's army was attacked by the enemy. The soldiers fought bravely but they were losing the battle. Suddenly they heard a shout.
"Follow me, brave men of China!"
Mu-lan was calling to the soldiers. They fought even more bravely, and before long the enemy fled. The soldiers cheered their brave leader, Mu-lan.

Mu-lan stayed in the army for ten more years. She won many battles and became a general. No one ever found out that she was a woman.

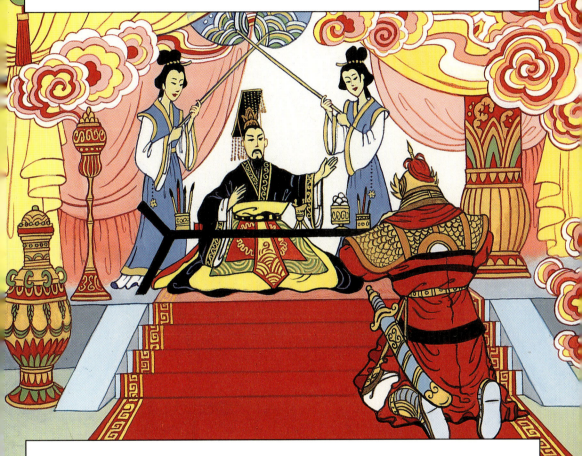

One day the emperor called Mu-lan to his palace. "Mu-lan, you have been a brave leader," he said. "I want to give you land and riches and an important job."

"Thank you," answered Mu-lan, "but all I really need is a strong camel to carry me. I want to go home to be with my father."

The emperor gladly gave Mu-lan the camel and sent two soldiers to travel with her. The journey was long and hard but at last they reached Mu-lan's village. News of her return spread quickly.
Red and gold lanterns were hung everywhere. The whole village was so proud of Mu-lan.

Mu-lan went to her home to take off her heavy armour.
She appeared in a beautiful dress. The two soldiers who rode with her could hardly believe their eyes.
"Our general is a *woman!*" they both exclaimed.

One of the soldiers went to Mu-lan and said, "All this time we have fought together, I have admired you so much. I never guessed you were a woman. I'd like to ask you to be my wife."

Mu-lan looked at him and answered,
"When I was your general, you honoured me.
Will you also honour me as your wife?"
The soldier gave his promise.
"Then I will marry you," Mu-lan replied.

Some months later the wedding took place.
Mu-lan wore a beautiful red dress.
Everyone in the village was invited
to the wedding feast.

Mu-lan and
her soldier husband
lived a long happy life.

Down through the years
the story of Mu-lan
has been told and
is still being told today.

Hilltown Star

A Fairy Tale Comes True

By Lynn Blanche
STAFF REPORTER
Illustrated by France Brassard

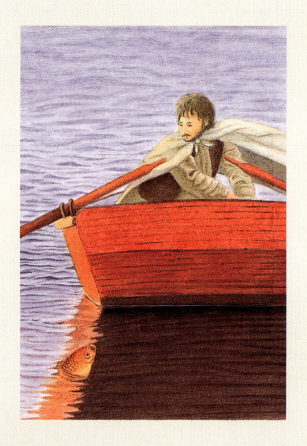

All children in Bosnia know the fairy tale about the poor man who caught a golden fish, let it go, and from then on had a happy life. This fairy tale came true for a woman and her two sons in a village in Bosnia.

It was 1992. The woman's husband had been away. When he returned to the village, he brought a special gift for his family—an aquarium with two golden fish.

Two years later, Bosnia was at war. The woman and her two sons had to flee to a safe place.

The father, who stayed behind to guard the village, was killed.

When the woman sneaked back into the village to bury her husband, she found the aquarium and the two golden fish. She took them to a lake nearby and set them free.

When the war ended, the woman and her sons returned to their village. They could not believe what they saw. The lake was full of golden fish!

The woman and her sons decided to feed the fish and sell them as a way to make money.

Now, in this Bosnian village, many homes and coffee shops have aquariums filled with golden fish.

Today, the family has a happy life and enough money to live well. "Our father gave us a very special gift," explains one of the sons.

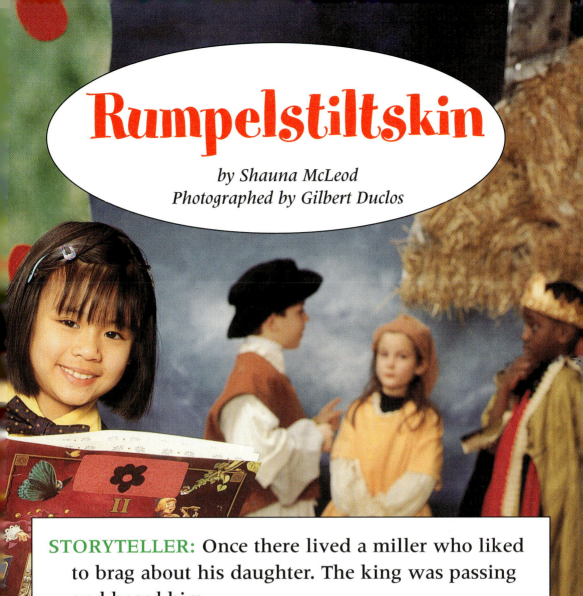

Rumpelstiltskin

by Shauna McLeod
Photographed by Gilbert Duclos

STORYTELLER: Once there lived a miller who liked to brag about his daughter. The king was passing and heard him.

MILLER: Last night my daughter Rose did something I can hardly believe. She spun straw into gold!

ROSE: Da-a-d!

KING: Excuse me, did you say straw into gold?

MILLER: That's right!

KING: Then, Rose, come to the castle and do the same for me!

STORYTELLER: Immediately, the king hurried Rose off to his castle. He took her to a room piled high with straw. In this room there was nothing but a chair and a spinning wheel.

KING: Okay, start spinning.

ROSE: Look, this is a mistake. My dad's so proud of me that he makes up . . .

KING: Never mind talking. Just spin this straw into gold by morning, or else . . .

AUDIENCE: Ooooohhhhh! You're in trouble!

ROSE: What am I going to do? I can't spin straw into gold!

[A LITTLE MAN leaps onto the stage.]

LITTLE MAN: I can!

ROSE: Who are you?

LITTLE MAN: Never mind that. What will you give me if I spin this straw into gold?
ROSE: I'll give you my necklace.
LITTLE MAN: Done!

STORYTELLER: With that, the little man sat down and started to spin. All through the night, he spun that straw. When the king came next morning, he could hardly believe his eyes. The straw had turned to shining gold.
KING: You are clever! Tonight you must spin more gold for me.
STORYTELLER: Poor Rose! The king put her in an even bigger room, with more straw piled even higher.

KING: Now, spin this straw into gold by morning, or else . . .

AUDIENCE: Oooooohhhh! Double trouble!

ROSE: Oh, if only that little man could help me again!

[The LITTLE MAN leaps onto the stage.]

LITTLE MAN: Here I am. What will you give me if I spin all this straw into gold?

ROSE: I'll give you my ring.

LITTLE MAN: Done.

STORYTELLER: He spun that straw into gold. When the king saw it, he took Rose to an even bigger room with even more straw piled even higher. Rose had nothing left to give the little man.

AUDIENCE: Oooooohhhhh! Triple trouble!

[The LITTLE MAN appears again.]

LITTLE MAN: Here's my deal. I'll spin this if you promise to give me your first child when you are queen.

ROSE: I'll never be queen!

LITTLE MAN: Just promise.

ROSE: Okay. I promise.

LITTLE MAN: Done!

STORYTELLER: When the king came in next day, he was delighted with the huge pile of gold.

KING: You are really clever! Please marry me.

ROSE: Oh! Well . . . yes.

STORYTELLER: So Rose became Queen. Years passed and Rose forgot about her promise. One day a baby prince was born. The little man appeared once again.

AUDIENCE: Oooooohhhh! Serious trouble!

LITTLE MAN: Well, Queen Rose! Remember the deal you made? I've come for your child.

ROSE: What! No, please don't take my baby!

LITTLE MAN: You promised!

ROSE: But I didn't think I'd ever be queen! Please! I'll give you all my jewels!

LITTLE MAN: No. A baby is more important to me than jewels.

ROSE: (*crying*) Please! Let me keep my baby.

LITTLE MAN: Here's my deal this time. If you can guess my name within three days, you can keep your baby.

STORYTELLER: Rose needed help—and fast! She called three messengers.

ROSE: I need names, boys' names, names to fit that little man.

STORYTELLER: The messengers searched the kingdom for names. The first two brought back a long list of names.

ROSE: Is your name Amal? Connor? Gordon?

LITTLE MAN: No, no, and no! And no more guesses today.

STORYTELLER: Next day, she made three more guesses.

ROSE: Well then, is it Alexander? Hector? Ivan?

LITTLE MAN: No, no, and NO! If you can't guess my name by tomorrow, the baby's mine!

(The **LITTLE MAN** *laughs gleefully and runs out of the room.*)

AUDIENCE: Oooohhhh! Rose, you're doomed!

STORYTELLER: It looked as if Rose would lose her baby . . . until the third messenger rushed in.

MESSENGER: Queen Rose, I think I've found your name. Last night, I saw a little man dancing around a fire and singing:

> *Fiddle, diddle, dance and sing,*
> *First a necklace, then a ring.*
> *Tricks and riddles are my game,*
> *RUMPELSTILTSKIN is my name!*

AUDIENCE: Oooohhhh! Yeah!

ROSE: Oh, thank you! Thank you!

(The **MESSENGER** *bows and leaves as the* **LITTLE MAN** *appears.)*

LITTLE MAN: I bet you still don't know my name. I'll take the baby now.

ROSE: Just a minute. I have three more guesses. Is your name Harwood? Is it . . . Percy? Is it . . . RUMPELSTILTSKIN?

(RUMPELSTILTSKIN *screams and falls to the floor in a temper tantrum.*)

RUMPELSTILTSKIN: That's not fair! Someone told you!

STORYTELLER: Now in the old fairy tale, Rumpelstiltskin made a terrible fuss. He stomped around so hard that his feet went through the floor and he disappeared forever. Here's how this tale ends.

AUDIENCE: Ohhhh?

(RUMPELSTILTSKIN *gets up, wipes his eyes, and sits by* ROSE.)

RUMPELSTILTSKIN: It's just that I've always wanted to have a baby brother to play with.

ROSE: Is that all you wanted? If you'd said that in the first place, we wouldn't have had all this trouble. You can visit anytime and play with my baby.

RUMPELSTILTSKIN: Do you really mean that?

ROSE: Of course. Come over every day, if you like.

STORYTELLER: Well, that's it. As they say, everyone lived happily ever after. When Queen Rose's baby grew up and became king, Rumpelstiltskin was right there.

AUDIENCE: Aaaaahhhh!